Sweet Home

MACRAMÉ

A BEGINNER'S GUIDE TO MACRAMÉ

Learn to make jewelry, home décor,
plant hangings, and more

CASEY ALBERTI

Walter Foster

Quarto.com
WalterFoster.com

© 2024 Quarto Publishing Group USA Inc.
Text © 2024 Casey Alberti

First Published in 2024 by Walter Foster Publishing, an imprint of
The Quarto Group, 100 Cummings Center, Suite 265-D, Beverly, MA
01915, USA. T (978) 282-9590 F (978) 283-2742

Walter Foster Publishing titles are also available at discount for retail,
wholesale, promotional, and bulk purchase. For details, contact
the Special Sales Manager by email at specialsales@quarto.com
or by mail at The Quarto Group, Attn: Special Sales Manager,
100 Cummings Center, Suite 265-D, Beverly, MA 01915, USA.

28 27 26 25 24   1 2 3 4 5

ISBN: 978-0-7603-8615-6

Digital edition published in 2024

eISBN: 978-0-7603-8616-3

Library of Congress Cataloging-in-Publication Data Available

Design: Kelley Galbreath
Cover Images: Casey Alberti; except back cover right image and
bottom left image, Christine Shields Photography
Page Layout: Kelley Galbreath
Photography: Casey Alberti, except Christine Shields Photography
on pages 4, 6, 30, 41, 47, 55, 65, 81, 105, 111, 117, 127

Printed in China

Contents

Introduction

HI THERE, AND THANK YOU for showing up! When I started my macramé journey, I would get so upset when I saw other makers copy my work and sell it as their own. I worked hard to find creative ways to revive this old craft, so it stung when I saw my work mimicked. But now, I've come full circle. I feel ready to retire from making and begin this new journey of teaching. I'm so excited to share my designs and can't wait to see all of your projects!

I began macramé as a simple idea for a girls' night. I quickly learned how to make a square knot and had so much fun teaching my girlfriends how to make some simple plant hangers. But it didn't stop there. I tried new patterns and techniques. Finally my husband asked me what in the world I was going to do with all these plant hangers lying around the house. I told him I'd sell them on Etsy and see what happens.

Well, a lot happened. After a year of perfecting the craft and coming up with my popular rainbow plant hanger designs, Etsy reached out to me to be featured on their blog. I still have no idea why they chose me or how they found me, but I was beyond excited. I prepped and planned but had no idea my shop would blow up the way that it did. Once the article came out, I worked seven days a week, twelve hours a day. I was burnt out! Now that I've found work-life balance, I'm ready to give my hands a rest and watch how macramé continues to evolve. I feel grateful to have found this art and love to watch others find their own way of styling it.

In this book you'll find color, and lots of it. And if you prefer neutrals, you're still in the right place! Every design can be customized by you to fit your needs and taste. For me, color is life. I love how I can use it to express myself, my mood, and my style. My hope is that these designs and colors inspire you to do the same.

I had a teacher once say, "perfect practice makes perfect," and that has stuck with me. Following the techniques and tips in this book will have you perfecting your art quickly, so you have time to find your own style. Be gentle with yourself as you learn, and remember to be bold. Who knows where this craft may take you!

Chapter One

Tools & Materials

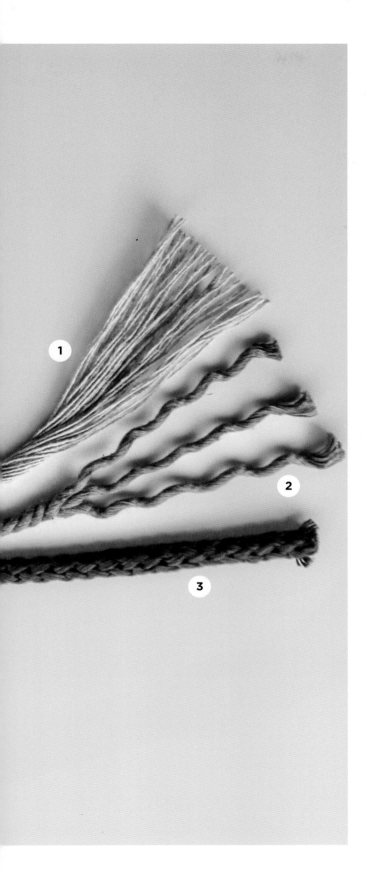

Cord & Rope

Macramé is measured in millimeters, which refers to the thickness. You can find cord as small as 1mm to as large as 16mm, and sometimes even thicker. Most projects are completed using 3 or 4mm cord.

Most macramé cords are made from cotton and come in three different types: single strand, 3-ply rope, and braided.

1 **Single Strand:** This is the most common cord type throughout this book. It's soft on the hands, easy to work with, and great for creating details.

2 **3-ply Rope:** Macramé rope is best for structure. Perfect for those heavy plants that need a sturdy hanger.

3 **Braided:** This cord type is also great for plant hangers and handbags. When looking for outdoor cord, look for a braided or 3-ply polypropylene cord.

No matter which type you purchase, I always recommend finding cord that's ethically sourced and has little to no dyes.

Supplies

MUST-HAVES

Scissors

Sharp scissors are an absolute nonnegotiable. You'll be doing so much cutting and trimming, you'll want a quality pair of scissors to make accurate and easy cuts.

Tape Measure

Measuring cord and distances between knots is essential. Any type of tape measure from your local craft or hardware store will do just fine.

Wood or Metal Rings

A necessary for those plant hangers. Metal rings give better piece of mind and are a must-have for heavier plants.

Pet Brush or Fine-Toothed Comb

To create fringe or tassels, you'll want something to easily brush out your single-strand cords.

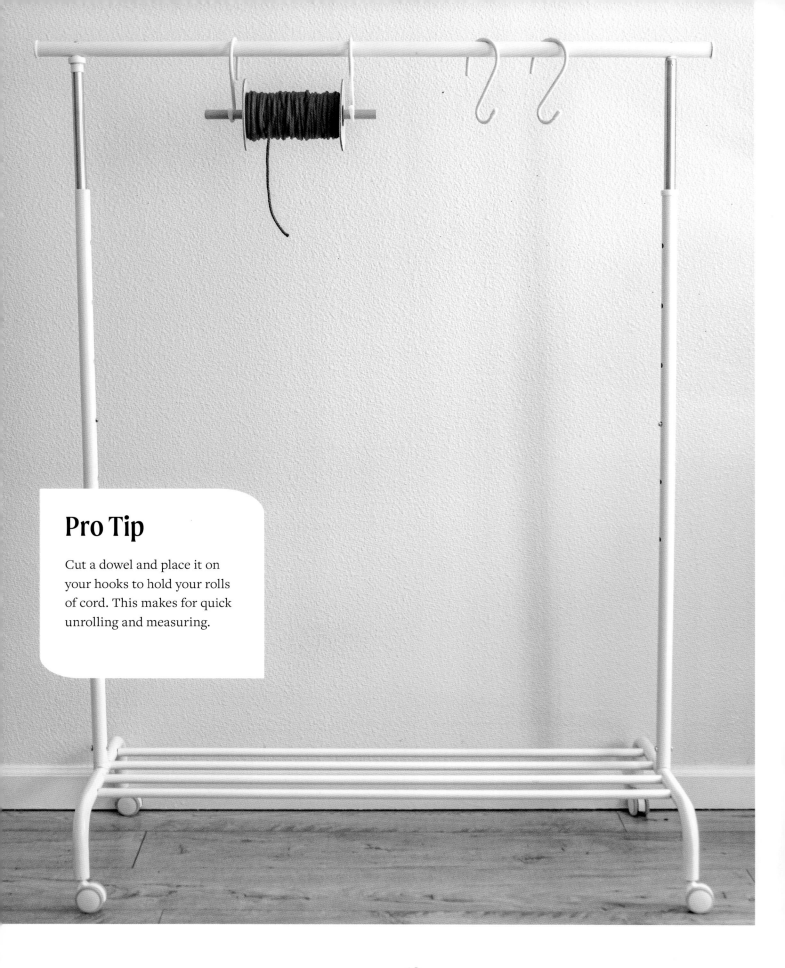

Pro Tip

Cut a dowel and place it on
your hooks to hold your rolls
of cord. This makes for quick
unrolling and measuring.

NICE-TO-HAVES

Clothes Rack

I found my first clothes rack on a marketplace for a few dollars and haven't been able to work without it. To save a ton of time, find a cheap rack with adjustable height. And when you become an expert maker, you can take it with you to hang your work at pop-up sales and markets.

S Hooks

These are important to hang your pieces on while you work. S hooks can be found on online marketplaces or your local hardware store. Be sure to buy a size that can fit nicely on your rack.

Cork Trivet & Push Pins

When making coasters, earrings, and more, these are an inexpensive and easy way to hold your work down.

Beads

Finding beads with holes large enough to thread macramé cords through can be tough. We'll have some fun later on with turning plain wood beads into something a little more eye-catching.

Crochet & Knitting Needles

You can find these at a big-box or local craft store. They aren't necessary but definitely make things easy when working in small spaces.

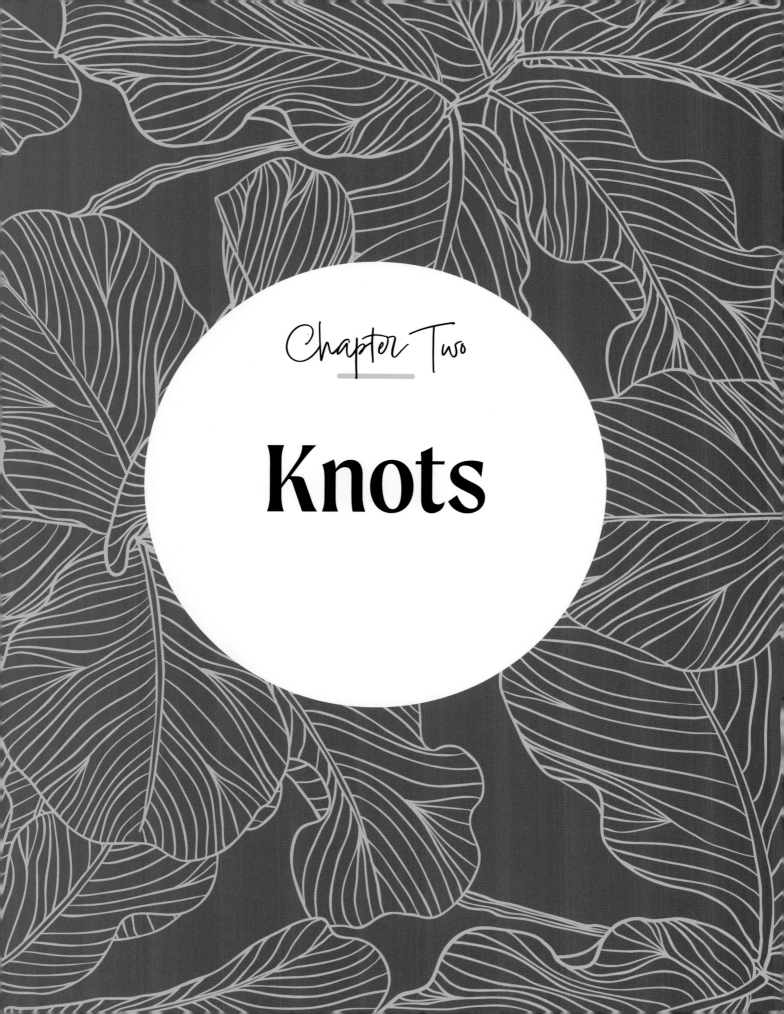

Chapter Two

Knots

Knotting How-to

LARK'S HEAD KNOT

The Lark's Head Knot is used to create attachments. It's normally done with one cord but can be done with more. This knot attaches macramé cord to dowels, rings, and other macramé cords. We'll be doing all three in the projects in this book.

One

Fold your cord in half, creating a loop in front of your dowel (or whatever you're attaching your cord to).

Two

Fold over your dowel and pull your cords through the loop.

Three

Pull down on your cords. Pull tight until secure. You can repeat this in the opposite direction for a different look.

Simply fold your cord in half, creating a loop behind your dowel, and repeat the steps to make the knot.

1

2

3a

3b

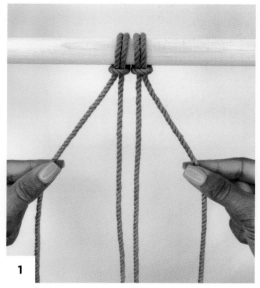

1

2

3

SQUARE KNOT

The square knot is likely the most common knot in macramé. It's often done with four cords but can be done with three or more. This knot is used on most projects and will be used the most throughout this book.

One

Working with four cords, grab the two outer cords.

Two

Cross the right cord over the center two, creating a backward number 4. The left cord goes on top of the right cord.

Three

Bring the left cord behind the center two cords.

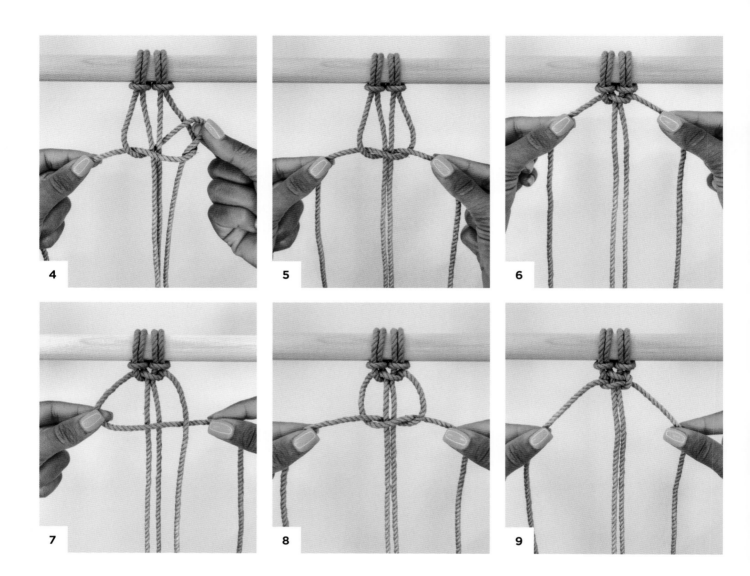

Four

Pull the left cord through the backward number 4 shape you created.

Five

The cords should be around the center two cords.

Six

Pull the two outer cords up and taut.

Seven

Repeat these steps in the opposite direction. Cross the left cord over the center two, creating a number 4 shape. The right cord goes on top of the left cord.

Eight

Pull the right cord through the 4 shape, with the cords around the center.

Nine

Pull up and taut. That's it—a square knot! You can continue this process to create a row of knots.

ALTERNATING SQUARE KNOTS

Alternating square knots are most common on plant hangers and wall hangings. They're perfect for creating structure and pattern.

One

Find the inner right cord and the inner left cord of your top row.

Two

Add a square knot.

Three

Find the outer left cord of your top row and the inner left cord of your second row. Add a square knot.

Four

Repeat on the other side, and continue to repeat this pattern.

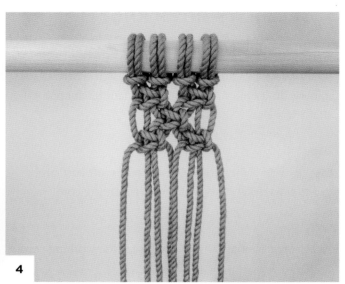

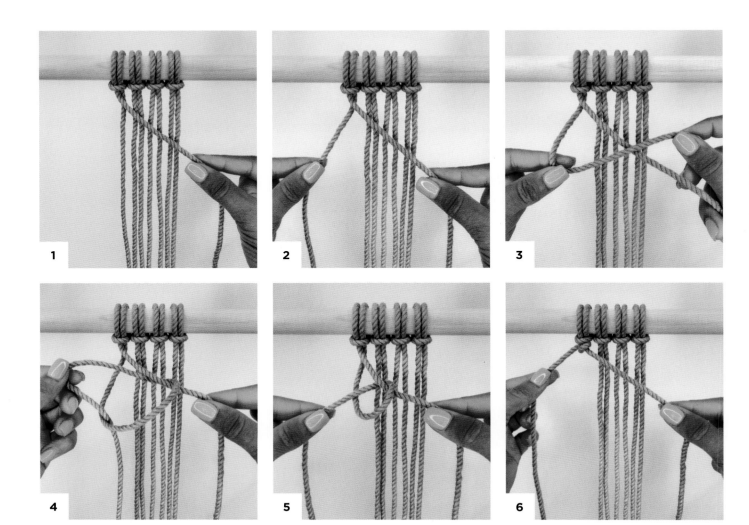

DOUBLE HALF HITCH KNOT

The double half hitch knot takes the most practice. Give yourself time and grace when perfecting this one. This knot is ideal when creating lines and design. There's really no limit on how interesting the half hitch knot can make a piece.

One

Starting with eight cords, find the outer left cord and hold at a diagonal. This will be your working cord.

Two

Find the next cord. It should be under the working cord.

Three

Bring this cord over the working cord, creating a number 4 shape.

Four

Wrap the cord around the working cord and thread through the 4 shape.

Five

Once through, pull to begin to tighten.

Six

Pull the cord tight and up and to the top of your work, keeping your working cord at a diagonal.

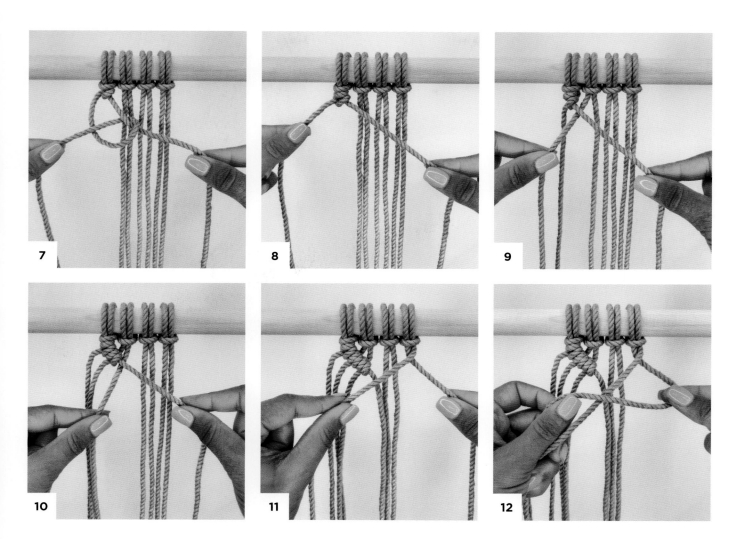

Seven

Repeat this process with the same working cord held at a diagonal.

Eight

Pull up and tighten under your last knot. You made a double half hitch knot! Hard work pays off!

Nine

Find the next cord and repeat this process, keeping your working cord held in the direction you want to go.

Ten

Find your next cord and repeat again. Half of your cords should now be in a diagonal line.

Eleven

Next repeat this on the other side. Find the outer right cord and hold at the same diagonal. This will be your working cord.

Twelve

Create a backward number 4 shape, with the cord coming over the working cord.

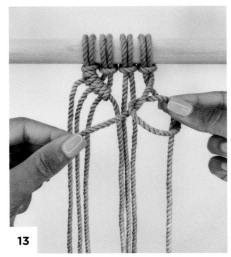

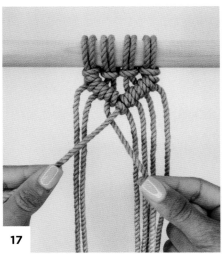
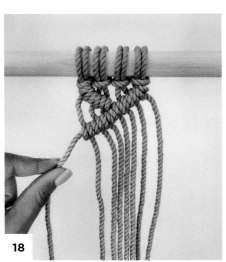

Thirteen

Wrap around and pull through the backward 4 shape.

Fourteen

Pull up and tighten.

Fifteen

Repeat this process with the same cord.

Sixteen

Working as on the other side, repeat the process to attach all your cords. Then attach your two working cords together. You can attach them going either direction, with the left cord being the working cord or the right. There is no wrong way.

Now that you've created the most common way of beginning a diamond pattern, let's continue.

Seventeen

Continuing with that same working cord you chose, find the next cord and continue the line.

Eighteen

After repeating the process, you should have one long diagonal line.

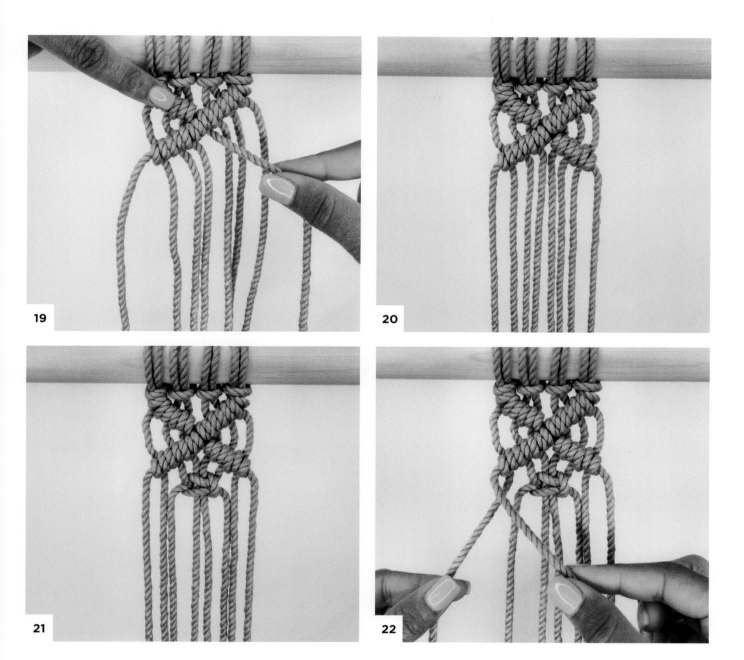

Nineteen

Find the working cord from your last line.

Twenty

Add a diagonal line of knots. You should have an "X" shape when you're done.

Twenty-One

Square knots are commonly added next, but it's not required.

Twenty-Two

Find your left working cord.

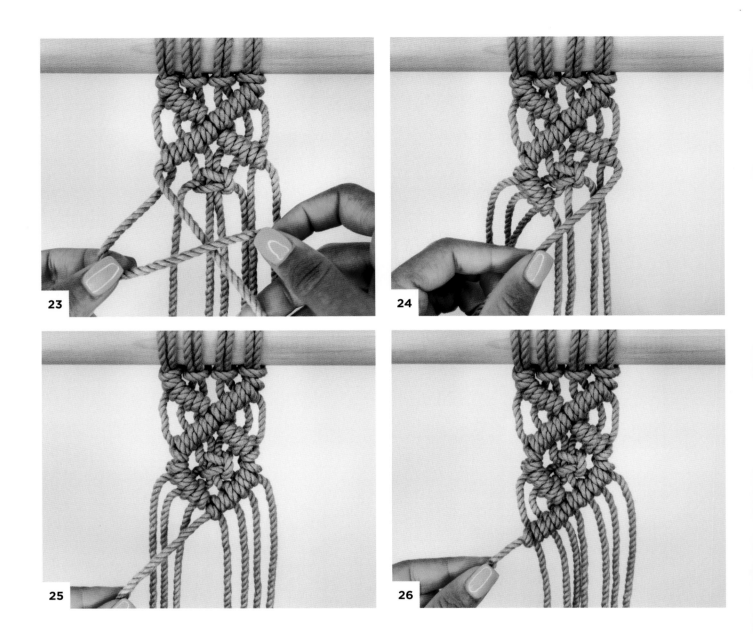

Twenty-Three

Begin adding double half hitch knots the same way you did previously.

Twenty-Four

Be sure to hold your working cord at the same angle as you did previously as you complete the line. Then find your right working cord.

Twenty-Five

Repeat the process, and attach your working cords. Make sure they are in same direction you did in the "X." This is an important step when creating the diamond pattern.

Twenty-Six

Repeat this process to continue adding diamonds.

HALF SQUARE KNOT: SPIRAL PATTERN

The half knot is a very popular macramé knot. Once you've mastered the square knot, this one is a breeze.

One

Start by working with the outer two cords.

Two

Complete the first half of a square knot.

Three

Instead of alternating to the other side, repeat the knot with the right cord going over the center cords.

Four

You should have two of the same knots.

Five

Repeat to continue this process. As you work, it will start to spiral on its own.

GATHERING KNOT

This knot is needed for plant hangers or to gather cords in other projects. You'll need one extra cord to complete your wraps.

One

Start by holding your cords in your hand.

Two

Place the end of your extra cord under your thumb.

Three

Loop the extra cord up, with about 2–3″ (5–7 cm) from the bottom of the loop to the top.

Four

Cross the long section of your cord over.

Five

Begin to wrap around tightly. As you wrap, make sure your cord is wrapping on top of your loop. Continue all the way around.

Six

Thread the end of the cord through the loop.

Seven

Pull up on your top cord to bring your loop and end under your wrapped cord.

Eight

Continue to pull up until your loop is about halfway under the wrapped cord. DO NOT PULL ALL THE WAY. Doing so will undo your work. Trim the end with scissors.

Nine

To hide the end, use the tip of your scissors or a small flathead screwdriver to push the end under the wrapped cord.

CONSTRICTOR KNOT

This knot is especially helpful when adding a hanging cord to wall hangings.

One

Wrap the short end of your cord over the dowel to the right.

Two

Wrap the short end of the cord around and up to the left, then down, creating an "X."

Three

Next you'll thread the end under the center of the "X."

Four

Thread the cord under the center of your "X."

Five

Pull both ends tight.

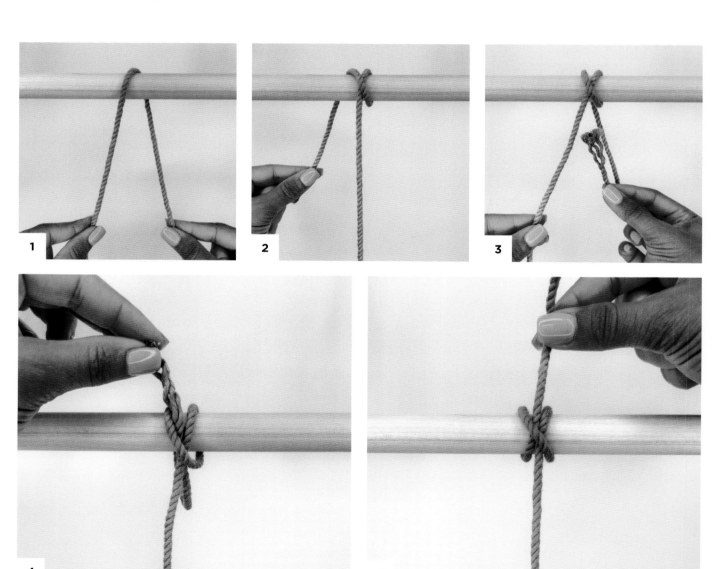

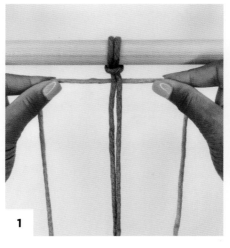
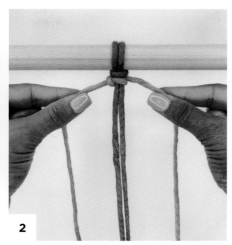
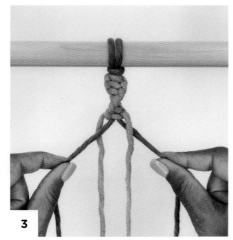
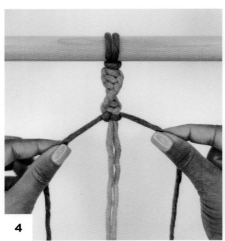
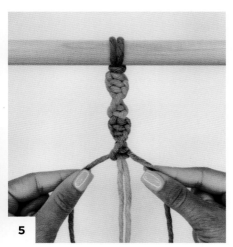
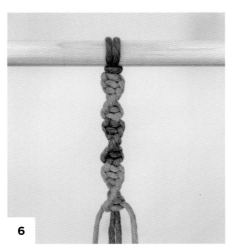

SWITCHING COLORS: SPIRAL PATTERN

One

At the halfway point of your first color, place the new color behind your cords.

Two

Add a half square knot over the cords.

Three

Continue your spiral pattern for as long as you like. To switch colors, bring the inner right cord behind and the inner left cord in front.

Four

Add a half square knot over the previous color.

Five

Continue your spiral pattern for as long as you like.

Six

Repeat the patterns. You can also do this process with the square knot.

Chapter Three

Designs

Sunset Wall Plant Hanger

This plant hanger will hold four small pots. The pots photographed are 4.5″ (11.4 cm) tall and 5″ (12.7 cm) in circumference.

Tools, Materials & Knots Needed

We'll be using 4mm zero-waste single strand cotton cord in this project. I've used the following:

Amour

Sunset

Apricot

Ocher

SUPPLIES:

Forty-eight 7½′ (2.3 m) cords, twelve of each color

Four 12″ (30.5 cm) cords, two amour & two apricot

Wood dowel ¾″ x 24″ (0.95 x 61 cm)

Scissors

Tape measure

Four small pots

OPTIONAL:

Garment rack

Two S hooks

Two cup hooks or two screws with anchors for hanging

KNOTS:

Lark's head knot

Alternating square knot

Double half hitch

Gathering knot

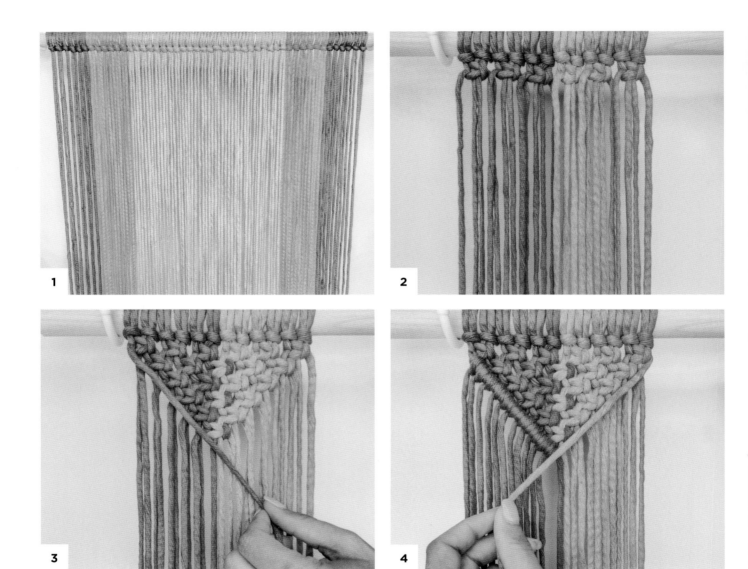

One

Add all your cords using lark's head knots. There should be six amour cords on the outside, followed by six sunset cords, then six apricot cords, and six ocher cords in the center. Make sure your middle ocher cord is centered on your dowel at 12″ (30.5 cm) in. Add your remaining cords in the same pattern.

Two

We'll start with the left twelve cords. Add a row of square knots.

Three

Add five additional rows of alternating square knots. You should have a "V" pattern. Using the far left amour cord as your working cord, add a line of double half hitch knots with the hanging amour cords, following the "V" shape.

Four

Use the far right sunset cord as your next working cord and add a row of double half hitch knots.

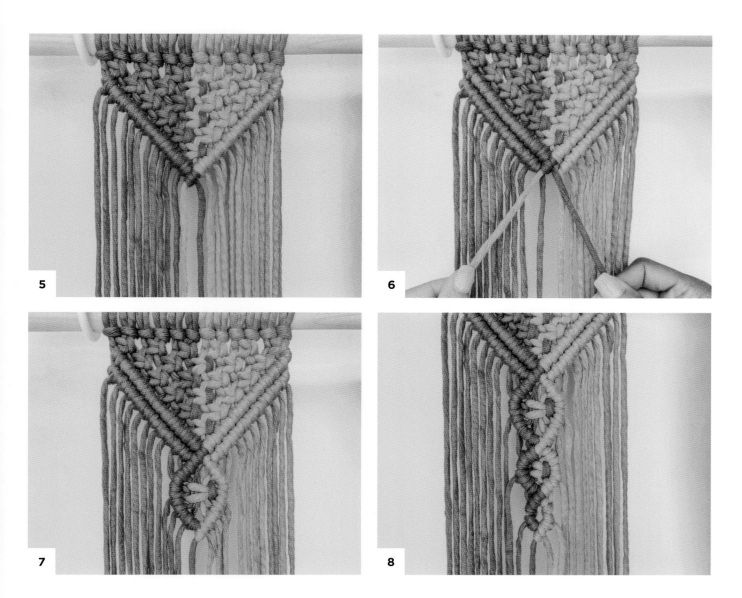

Five

Attach the working cords with a double half hitch knot.

Six

Repeat these steps to add another line of double half hitch knots, but do not attach these working cords. Then find your first set of working cords.

Seven

Add a diamond pattern with the three hanging cords on each side. Add a square knot inside your diamond.

Eight

Add a diamond pattern with the two hanging cords on each side. Add a square knot inside your diamond. Then add a diamond pattern with the one hanging cord on each side.

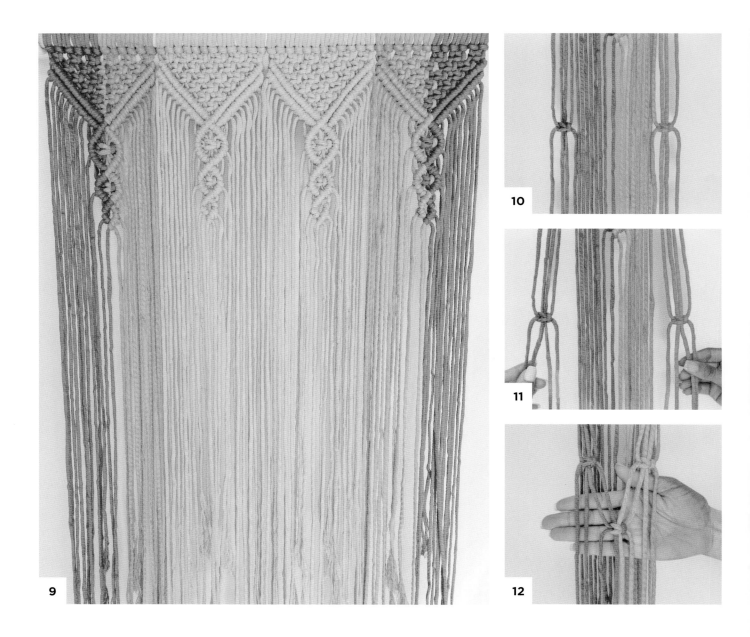

Nine

Repeat steps two through eight with each set of twelve cords. You should have four sections.

Ten

Measuring 12½″ (31.8 cm) from your dowel, add a square knot with your outer four amour cords. Repeat this with the outer four sunset cords.

Eleven

Find the outer two cords of the square knots.

Twelve

Bring them around and toward each other and add an alternating square knot 2″ (5 cm) down from your first row.

Thirteen

Find the next set of two hanging cords.

Fourteen

Add another square knot, ensuring it's even with your center knot. Repeat on the other side. You should have two rows of alternating square knots.

Fifteen

Add another row of alternating square knots 1" (2.5 cm) below your second row. You should have three rows of alternating square knots.

Sixteen

Repeat steps ten through fifteen on each section.

Seventeen

Turn your work around. Using your center four hanging cords, add a square knot at the same level as your front second row.

Add another row of alternating square knots at the same level as your front third row.

Eighteen

Add a third row of alternating square knots directly below your second row. Add a square knot in the center about ½" (1.3 cm) below.

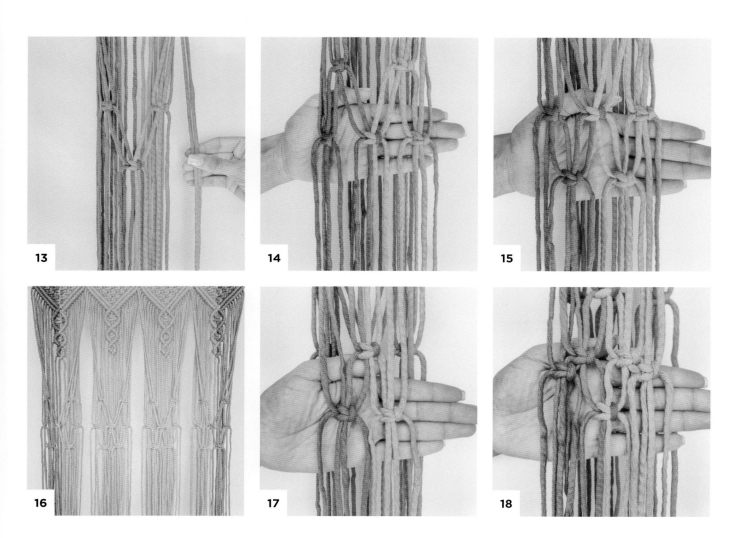

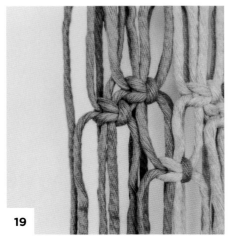

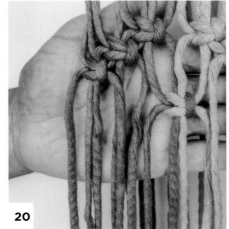

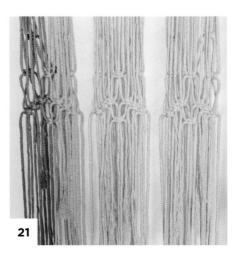

Nineteen

Next you'll attach your front and back. Find the hanging two cords from your front second row.

Twenty

Add a square knot directly below your third row.

Twenty-One

Repeat this on each section.

Twenty-Two

Gather the cords of one section and add a pot, leveling it where you desire. Ensure you hold the gathering toward the back of the pot, as shown, not in the center.

Twenty-Three

Remove the pot without removing your hand. Add a gathering knot and add the pot back. Gather the cords of the next section and add a pot, making sure the two pots are level to each other. Remove the pot and add a gathering knot. Repeat this on each section. Turn your work back around. Trim where desired.

Personalize Your Piece

How can you make this piece your own? I've made this piece in lots of different colorways. If you want to try a rainbow colorway, you'll need eight cords in each color. Or, if neutrals would go well in your space, try out taupe and ivory. Solid forest green with gold gathering knots would be stunning. Having fun with color in the piece is key!

Black & Rainbow Plant Hanger

This plant hanger will hold a medium-sized pot. The pot photographed is 5½″ (14 cm) tall and 5″ (12.7 cm) in circumference.

Tools, Materials & Knots Needed

We'll be using 4mm zero-waste single strand cotton cord in this project. I've used the following:

Red amber

Copper

Ocher

Forest

Navy

Eggplant

Black

SUPPLIES:

Twelve 16″ (40.6 cm) cords, two of each rainbow color

Six 48″ (122 cm) cords, 1 of each rainbow color

Six 7.5′ (2.3 m) cords, black

Wood ring

Scissors

Tape measure

OPTIONAL:

Small flathead screwdriver

Garment rack

S hook

KNOTS:

Gathering knot

Alternating square knot

One

Thread the black cords through your ring, ensuring they are even at the ends.

Two

Using one of your 16″ (40.6 cm) red amber cords, add a gathering knot below your ring. Wrap the cord around four times and trim the ends.

Three

Repeat this process with your remaining cords, working in rainbow order. I like to use a small flathead screwdriver to tuck away the ends. You can also use the tips of your scissors to push down the ends, hiding them under your gathering knots.

Four

Turn your work around. Use your 48″ red amber cord to add a square knot to the left two black hanging cords, 16″ (40.6 cm) from the bottom of your purple gathering knot. You can slide your square knot up or down if desired.

Five

Repeat with your copper and ocher cords, ensuring they are even with each other. Add a row of alternating black square knots 3″ (7.6 cm) down.

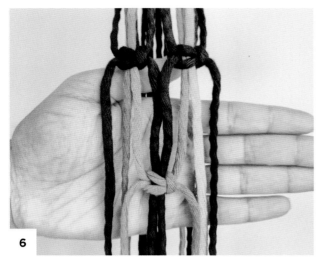

Six

Add a square knot in the third row 2″ (5 cm) down.

Seven

Turn your work around. Add your forest, navy, and eggplant cords and complete the alternating square knots. Your work should all be connected with three rows of alternating square knots.

Eight

Gather all your cords. Using your remaining eggplant and navy cords, add a gathering knot 1½″ (3.8 cm)

from your last set of square knots. Trim two of your colored cords, leaving about 1″ (2.5 cm). It does not matter which colors.

Trim a second set of cords slightly below the last. Continue doing this, being careful not to cut any black cords.

Nine

Continue adding your gathering knots in opposite rainbow order. Once you add copper, trim any remaining colored cords if they're too long, and tuck in the ends.

Pro Tip

If you'd like to use a smaller pot, shorten the distance between your alternating square knots. For larger pots, lengthen the distance between the square knots.

Neutral-Colored Coasters

These coasters will measure about 5″ (12.7 cm) in diameter. If needed, clean with a damp cloth using mild soap and warm water.

Tools, Materials & Knots Needed

We'll be using 4mm zero-waste single strand cotton cord in this project. I've used the following:

Olive

Ivory

Oat

SUPPLIES:

One 46″ (117 cm) cord, olive

Three 28″ (71 cm) cords, olive

Three 28″ (71 cm) cords, ivory

Three 18″ (45.7 cm) cords, olive

Three 18″ (45.7 cm) cords, oat

Three 11″ (27.9 cm) cords, olive

Three 11″ (27.9 cm) cords, oat

Cork trivet

Pushpins

Pet brush or fine-tooth comb

Scissors

Tape measure

OPTIONAL:

Fabric stiffener

Hot glue gun

KNOTS:

Lark's head knot

Double half hitch knot

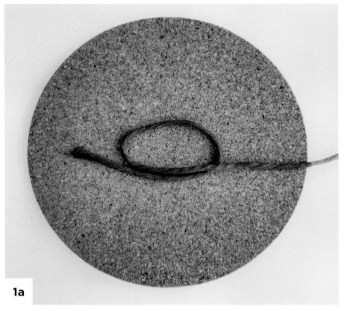

1a

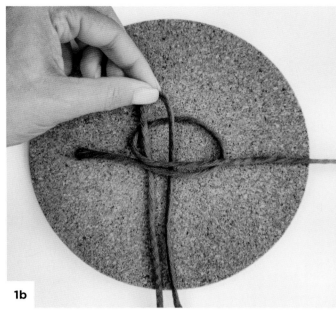

1b

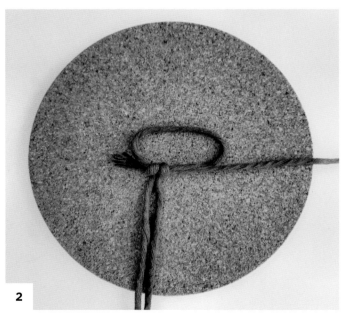

2

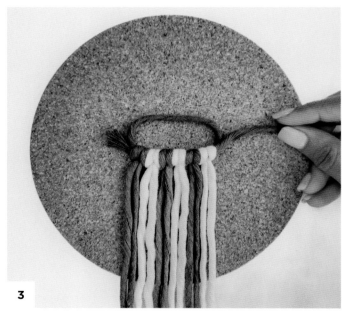

3

One

Start by looping the end of your 46″ (117 cm) olive cord over itself, ensuring the end of the cord is under the longer section. This will be your working cord. Thread one of your 28″ (71 cm) olive cords under the stacked section of your loop.

Two

Attach it using the lark's head knot.

Three

Repeat with the ivory cord, and continue alternating the colors with your 28″ (71 cm) cords.

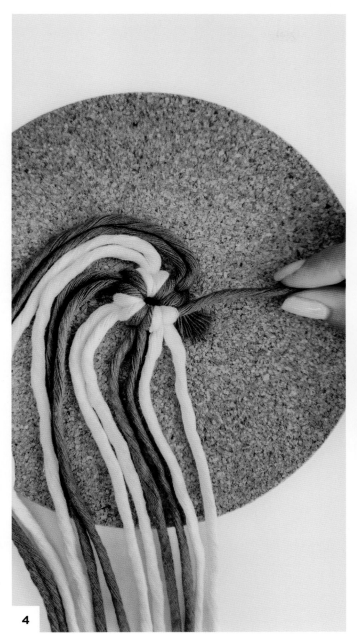

Four

Pull the working cord, which closes your loop. Do not lose your short end. You can pull on it also to further tighten your loop.

Five

Pin your work to the cork. This is an important step! Your working cord should always be on top of your remaining cords.

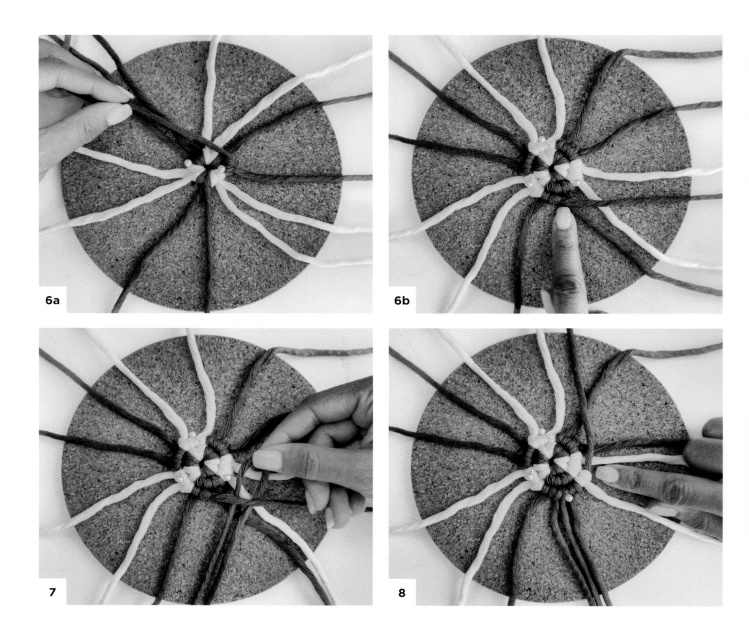

Six

Starting with the first olive cord to the right of your working cord, add a double half hitch knot. Continue this all the way around. Move your pins around as you work to prevent your work from curling up into a bowl shape.

Once you have gotten back to where you started, there will be a gap in the middle of the two olive cords.

Seven

Thread one of your 18″ (45.7 cm) olive cords under your working cord.

Eight

Attach the cord using a lark's head knot, and continue your double half hitch knots. There will be a gap in the middle of the two ivory cords.

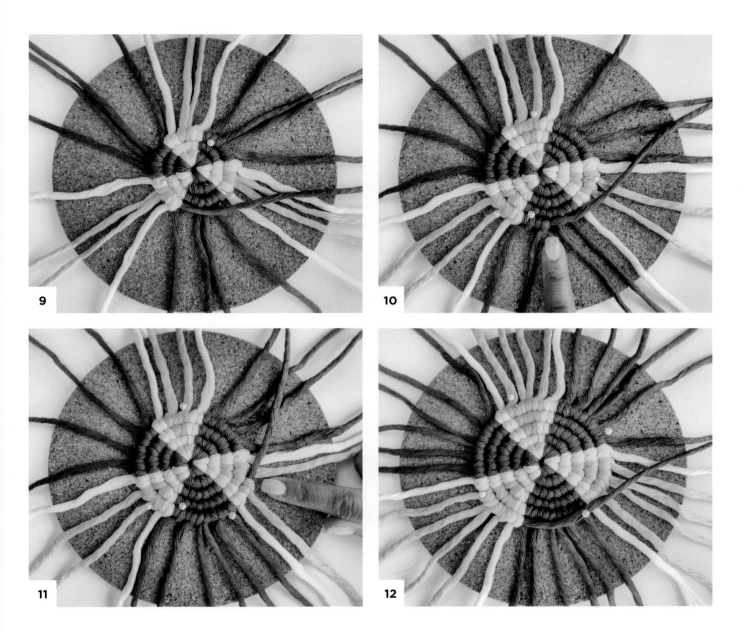

Nine

Add one of your 18″ (45.7 cm) oat cords using a lark's head knot. Continue this process, adding your remaining 18″ (45.7 cm) cords.

Ten

Go around one more time without adding any cords. There will be a gap in the center of your olive section. Add one of your 11″ (27.9 cm) olive cords here.

Eleven

Continue your double half hitch knots. Then add one of your 11″ (27.9 cm) cords to the center of your oat section.

Twelve

Continue this process, adding your remaining 11″ (27.9 cm) cords.

Pro Tip

Add a few drops of hot glue on the bottom of the coaster to keep it from sliding on your coffee table.

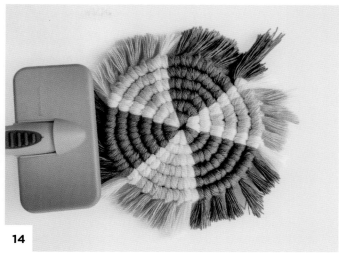

Thirteen

Go around one more time without adding any cords. Trim the fringe, using your fingers as the length measurement.

> **Tip:** For a perfect measure, there are cutting guides available to use with a rotary cutter.

Fourteen

Using your pet brush or comb, brush out the fringe.

Fifteen

If you are not using fabric stiffener, evenly trim again once brushed out. If you are using fabric stiffener, spray it on, brush again, and let dry before trimming the ends evenly.

Light Green Air Plant Hanger

Once hung, this small hanging will measure about 13″ (33 cm) in length.

Tools, Materials & Knots Needed

We'll be using 4mm zero-waste single strand cotton cord in this project. I've used the following:

Agave

Ivory

SUPPLIES:

Ten 5′ (1.5 m) cords, agave

Two 12″ (30.5 cm) cords, ivory

One 12″ (30.5 cm) cord, agave

One 24″ (61 cm) cord, agave

Wood dowel, ⅝″ x 6″ (1.6 x 15.2 cm)

Scissors

Tape measure

OPTIONAL:

Crochet needle

Garment rack

Two S hooks

KNOTS:

Lark's head knot

Alternating square knot

Double half hitch knot

Gathering knot

Constrictor knot

One

Add all your 5′ (1.5 m) agave cords to your dowel using lark's head knots. Then add a row of square knots.

Two

Add four additional rows of alternating square knots, creating a "V" pattern. The far right cord will be your working cord.

Three

Add a line of double half hitch knots with the hanging cords, following the "V" shape. Repeat on the other side. Then place your ivory cord behind your far left hanging cord.

4

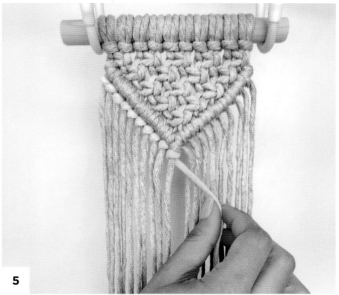

5

6

Four

Place the end of the ivory cord in your right hand over the top of your hanging cord, and wrap it behind the hanging cord. Slide up to the bottom of your double half hitch knots.

Five

Wrap the cord around your next hanging cord, and repeat with all the cords on the left.

Six

Using the far left agave cord as your working cord, add a line of double half hitch knots with the hanging cords, following the "V" shape.

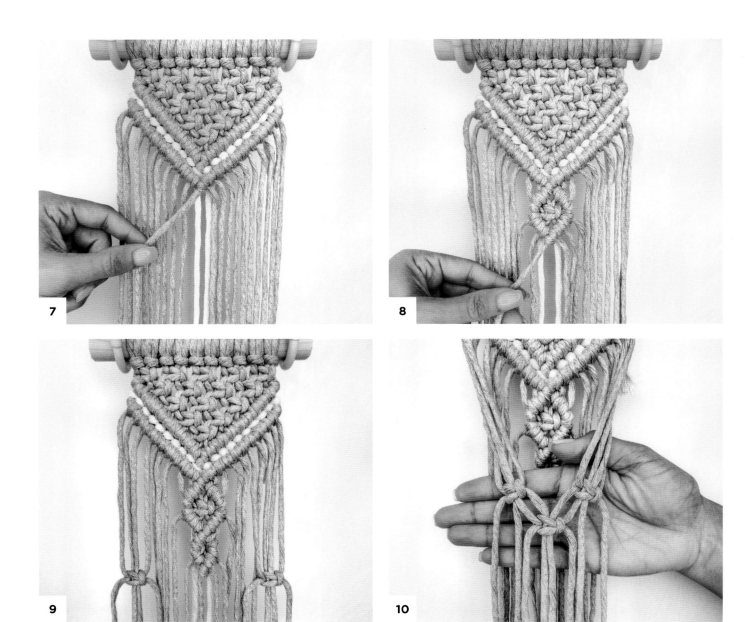

Seven

Repeat steps four to six on the right side. You will continue with this working cord in the next step.

Eight

Add a diamond pattern using the two hanging cords on each side. Add a square knot to the inside of your diamond.

Nine

Add a diamond pattern using the one hanging cord on each side. Then add a square knot with the far left cords 6½″ (16.5 cm) from your dowel. Repeat on the other side.

Ten

Bring the outer two cords of each square knot around and together, and add a square knot about ½″ (1.3 cm) below your top row.

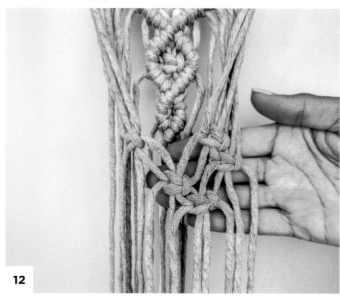

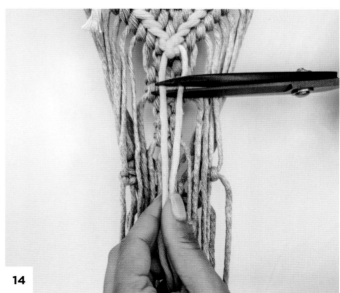

Eleven

Next you'll attach the back to the front. Find the outer two hanging back cords on the right.

Twelve

Add a square knot directly below your top row, followed by another square knot directly below your third row.

Thirteen

Repeat this on the other side.

Fourteen

Turn your work around. Knot your ivory cords together and trim them, leaving about ½″ (1.3 cm).

15

16

Fifteen

Find your center four cords and add a square knot at the same level as your front second row.

Sixteen

Add another row of square knots directly below your first knot. Now you'll attach the front and back. Start by finding your outer right cords from the last row on your front side.

Seventeen

Attach the cords with a square knot to your bottom row.
There should be four cords inside of your knot. Repeat
this on the other side.

Eighteen

Add a gathering knot directly below your last row of
square knots with your 12″ (30.5 cm) agave cord. Trim
where desired.

20

21

Nineteen

Now you'll attach the 24″ (61 cm) agave cord to the dowel. Attach with a constrictor knot.

Twenty

Thread the end of the cord through your needle. Slide the needle under a few of your lark's head knots.

Twenty-One

Pull through. Add a knot to the end and trim. Repeat on the other side.

Personalize Your Piece

You can have fun with this little cutie in tons of other colorways. To add some texture, maybe try weaving in a braided cord or silk in your "V" shape.

Green & Gold Wall Hanging

This piece will measure 24″ (61 cm) wide and about 32″ (81 cm) long. However, it's a good idea to remain open to adjustments.

Tools, Materials & Knots Needed

We'll be using 2mm zero-waste 3-ply cotton rope in this project. I've used the following:

Forest

SUPPLIES:

Sixty 10′ (3 m) cords

Gold crochet thread

Three wood dowels, ¼″ x 24″ (0.63 x 61 cm)

One wood dowel, ½″ x 23½″ (1.3 x 59.7 cm)

Gold spray paint

Forty-seven gold tube beads (30 x 4 mm)

Gold leaf & gilding adhesive

Natural bristle paintbrush & nylon paintbrush

Scissors

Tape measure

OPTIONAL:

Hot glue gun

Garment rack

Two S hooks

KNOTS:

Lark's head knot

Double half hitch knot

Alternating square knot

Gathering knot

Skip ahead to the end for a lesson on miscalculation and an alternate ending.

One

Spray paint your ½″ (1.3 cm) dowel and let dry. Add a lark's head knot with a group of ten cords.

Repeat this adding five more groups of ten cords, spacing your lark's head knots about 2″ (5 cm) apart. You should have six knots evenly spaced on your dowel. (See step twelve for the full six groups of cords on dowel.)

Two

Next you'll add one of your ¼″ (0.63 cm) dowels about 3″ (7.6 cm) below your top dowel. Find the far right cord from your first section. Add two beads to the cord.

Three

Pull the cord around and up over the dowel, wrapping around the dowel to the left. Bring it up again, leaving a loop. Wrap the cord around the back of the dowel.

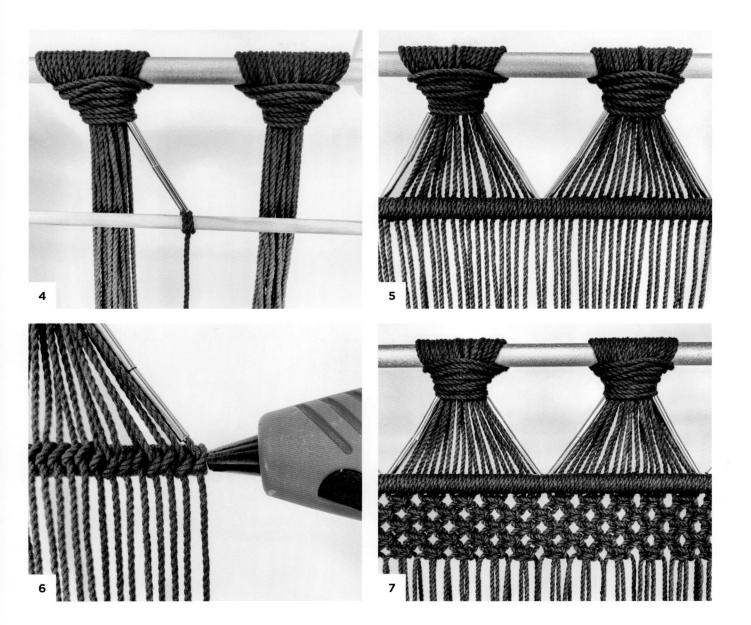

Four

Thread the end through the loop and pull tight.

Five

Repeat these steps, adding the beads to the far right and left cords of each section, and attaching all the cords without beads in the center to the dowel.

Six

Add a bead of hot glue under the last knot on each side.

Seven

Add five rows of alternating square knots directly below your dowel.

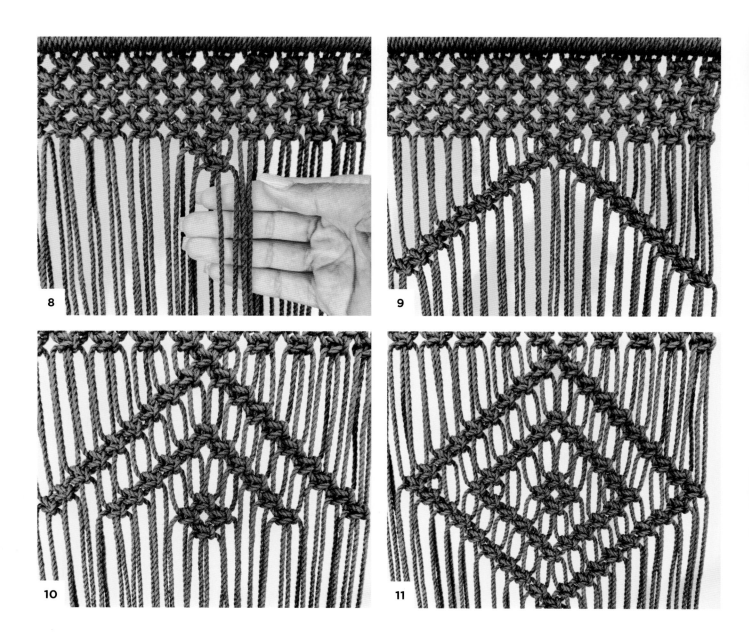

Eight

Find the four cords directly below the middle of two lark's head sections, and begin adding alternating square knots diagonally to the right.

Nine

Continue until you have ten knots. Then repeat this going to the left.

Ten

Add a second row, with the top knot at the same level as the fifth knot of your outer triangle. Then add a diamond pattern of square knots, with the top knot at the same level as the fifth knot of your second triangle.

Eleven

Finish the diamonds with alternating square knots in the opposite direction.

Twelve

Repeat steps eight through eleven to add two more diamond sections between the other groups of lark's head knots.

Thirteen

Add another five rows of alternating square knots. Then add another dowel below your square knots, just as in steps three and four.

Fourteen

Turn your piece around. Gather twenty of the hanging cords and add a gathering knot with your crochet thread 3¾″ (9.5 cm) below your dowel. This gathering knot should be about ½″ (1.3 cm) tall. Repeat this with each group of ten cords, ensuring your gathering knots are level with each other. Then turn your work back around.

Fifteen

Add your last dowel, ensuring your gathering knots are centered between the two dowels. Then add three rows of alternating square knots.

Sixteen

Measuring 1½″ (3.8 cm) down from your knots, add a bead of hot glue. Add two beads and let dry.

Seventeen

Continue adding beads in your desired pattern. I chose to add my beads in a stairstep pattern every 1½″ (3.8 cm). Trim your ends below your beads.

Eighteen

Turn your work over. Cut 10″ (25.4 cm) cords to hot glue on the backside of your dowel. It's best to add four to five cords at a time.

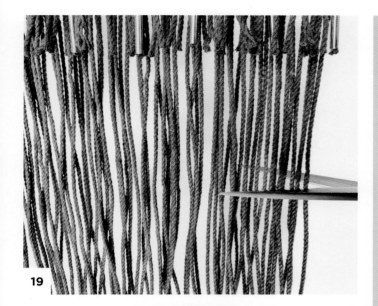

19

20

Dealing with Miscalculations

Full transparency time! This piece didn't turn out how I imagined it in my head. My goal was to add several more rows of square knots at the bottom and repeat the diamond patterns, but I realized that I measured my cord wrong. This happens pretty frequently in macramé, even to expert makers. When creating something new, I always write down my cord measurements so when I re-create it, I know exactly what I need. I also always try to keep an open mind and come up with creative solutions when things don't go as planned.

To create this piece as I originally intended, cut your sixty cords at 15′ (4.6 m). Repeat the diamond section and add another dowel at the end. How'd it turn out?

Nineteen

Continue cutting cords as you need them, and continue all the way across your work. Trim the ends where desired or add a third row to add another layer.

Twenty

If needed, trim the wood ends off your dowels for a clean look. Apply the gilding adhesive to the cords in between your diamond patterns. Let dry until tacky to the touch.

Then add your gold leaf following the package instructions. Repeat this on each diamond section. Brush excess gold leaf off with a paintbrush.

Crystal Rainbow Plant Hanger

Though not required, this beautiful piece would look best with a rounded, medium-sized pot. The pot photographed is 5½″ (14 cm) tall and 7½″ (19 cm) in circumference.

Tools, Materials & Knots Needed

We'll be using 4mm zero-waste single strand cotton cord in this project. I've used the following:

Red amber

Copper

Ocher

Forest

Navy

Eggplant

Black

SUPPLIES:

Twelve 16′ (4.9 m) cords, two of each rainbow color

Six 5′ (1.5 m) cords, one of each rainbow color

Two 18″ (45.7 cm) cords, black

Twenty-seven octagon crystals with jump rings

Metal ring

Scissors

Tape measure

OPTIONAL:

Beads

Small flathead screwdriver

Garment rack

S hook

KNOTS:

Gathering knot

Double half hitch knot

Lark's head knot

Alternating square knot

One

Thread the rainbow cords through your ring in rainbow order, as shown. Ensure they are even at the ends. Use one of your black cords to add a gathering knot below your ring. Trim the ends, hiding them with your screwdriver or the tip of your scissors.

Two

Starting with the far left red amber cord, add double half hitch knots with your remaining red amber cords.

Starting with the far right copper cord, add double half hitch knots with your remaining copper cords. Close your "V" shape.

Three

Continue your double half hitch knots, creating the top of your diamond pattern. If desired, you can add a square knot instead of using crystals, as shown.

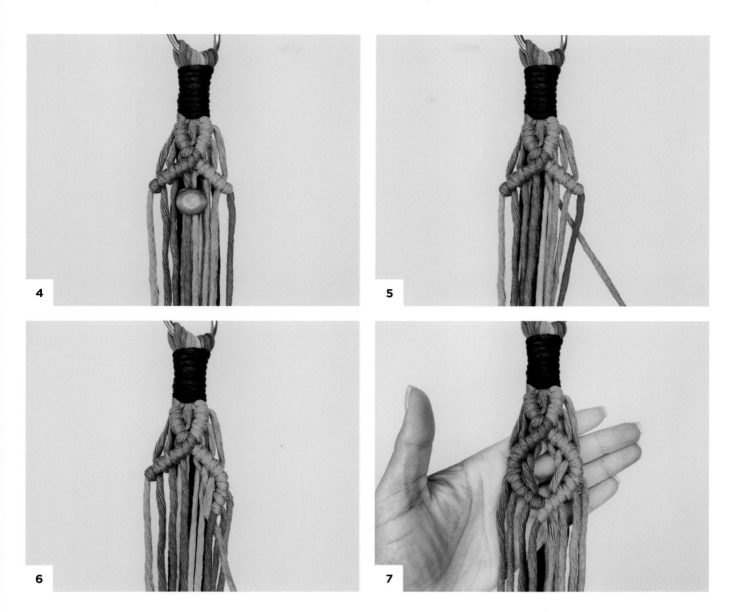

Four

Alternatively, you can use beads that you have on hand. You'll need twenty-seven beads if you choose this route.

Five

If using crystals, you'll continue your double half hitch knots. Begin the bottom half of the diamond pattern, first with the inner copper cord, and attach from behind your remaining copper cords.

Six

Repeat this with the next copper cord, ensuring you bring it from behind your remaining copper cords. Finish with the third remaining copper cord.

Seven

Repeat this on the red amber side. Attach the sides.

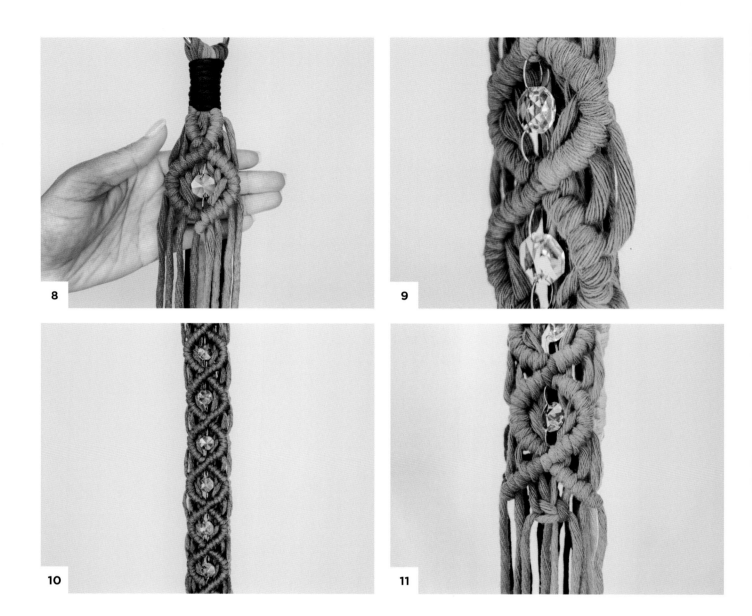

Eight

Attach the jump rings of your crystal to the cords on the inner top and bottom of your diamond.

Nine

Repeat this process until you have nine crystals.

Ten

Repeat steps two through nine with your ocher-and-forest and navy-and-eggplant sides.

Eleven

Add the top of the diamond pattern on each side. Add a square knot inside.

Twelve

Attach your copper 5′ (1.5 m) cords with lark's head knots on the working cord, spacing them about ½″ (1.3 cm) apart from each other. Repeat this with your red amber cords.

13

14

15

Thirteen

Add a row of alternating square knots at the level of your lark's head knots. Add another row of square knots, and repeat until you have five rows.

Fourteen

Repeat steps twelve and thirteen on each side. Attach copper and ocher at the bottom of your last lark's head knots with a square knot directly below the lark's head knots. Repeat this with each section.

Fifteen

Add two more rows of alternating square knots all the way around your work, ensuring they are all level. Gather all your cords and add your pot.

Remove the pot while still holding your cords. Add a gathering knot using your remaining black cord. Put the pot back to ensure you like its placement.

Moody Lampshade

This lampshade will measure about 13″ (33 cm) in length.
Feel free to substitute cord color(s) and beading.

Tools, Materials & Knots Needed

We'll be using using 4mm zero-waste single strand cotton cord in this project. I've used the following:

Black

SUPPLIES:

108 80″ (274.3 cm) cords, black

Six 12″ (30.5 cm) crochet thread strings

Forty-eight wood beads

12″ (30.5 cm)-diameter metal drum shade, top & bottom

Pet brush or fine-tooth comb

Scissors

Tape measure

OPTIONAL:

Garment rack

Two or three S hooks

Rose gold spray paint

KNOTS:

Lark's head knot

Double half hitch knot

One

Spray paint your beads, if desired, and set them aside to dry. Fold a cord in half and place the loop behind your ring. Attach with a lark's head knot.

Two

Repeat to add two more cords. Each pattern will be done with three cords. Begin your half hitch knots moving in a diagonal to the right.

Three

Switch directions and continue your half hitch knots to the left. Be sure the angles are even with each other. Then switch directions again to continue to the right.

Four

Continue this process until you have four corners on the left and four on the right. Next you'll attach your bottom ring with the cords on the inside of the ring.

4

5

6

Pro Tip

Your bottom half hitch knots may not always want to fit, especially if your top ring and bottom ring are the same diameter. It's okay to skip a few cords at the bottom if needed.

Five

Attach each cord using a double half hitch knot, making sure they are squeezed in together.

Six

Attach your next set of three cords and repeat the pattern in the opposite direction.

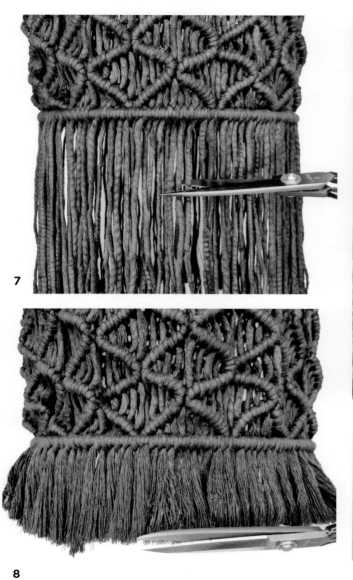

Seven

Continue repeating the pattern with your remaining cords. Trim your ends where desired.

Eight

Brush out the fringe with a pet brush or fine-tooth comb. Trim again, measuring around the work to ensure the ends are even.

Nine

String eight beads onto your crochet thread. You can also use macramé cord if needed. Tie the thread to the bottom ring every four and a half sections.

Repeat this all the way around your work. Trim again if needed.

Black & Rose Gold Wall Hanging

The fun part about this piece is it mixes a traditional macramé wall hanging pattern with so many options to be creative with color, beading, and shimmers.

Tools, Materials & Knots Needed

We'll be using black 4mm zero-waste single strand cotton cord in this project. I've used the following:

Black

SUPPLIES:

Twenty-four 15' (4.6 m) cords

Four 12½' (3.8 m) cords

Twenty 41" (104 cm) cords

Wood dowel, ¾" x 32" (1.9 x 81.3 cm)

Fifteen 20mm wood beads

Rose gold spray paint

Rose gold leaf & gilding adhesive

Natural bristle paintbrush & nylon paintbrush

Scissors

Tape measure

OPTIONAL:

Garment rack

Two S hooks

Two cup hooks or two screws with anchors for hanging

KNOTS:

Lark's head knot

Double half hitch knot

Half square knot

One

Apply a thin layer of gilding adhesive to the length of one side of the dowel. Let dry until the adhesive is clear and feels tacky to the touch. Apply the gold leaf following the package instructions.

Repeat until the entire dowel is covered. Spray paint your beads and set aside to dry. Brush the excess gold leaf off.

Two

Using your 15′ (4.6 m) cords, add two sections of four cords using the lark's head knot. The sections should be about 8″ (20.3 cm) apart.

Three

Starting on the left section, begin your double half hitch knots to the right. Create a "V" shape. Attach the working cords and continue to the right.

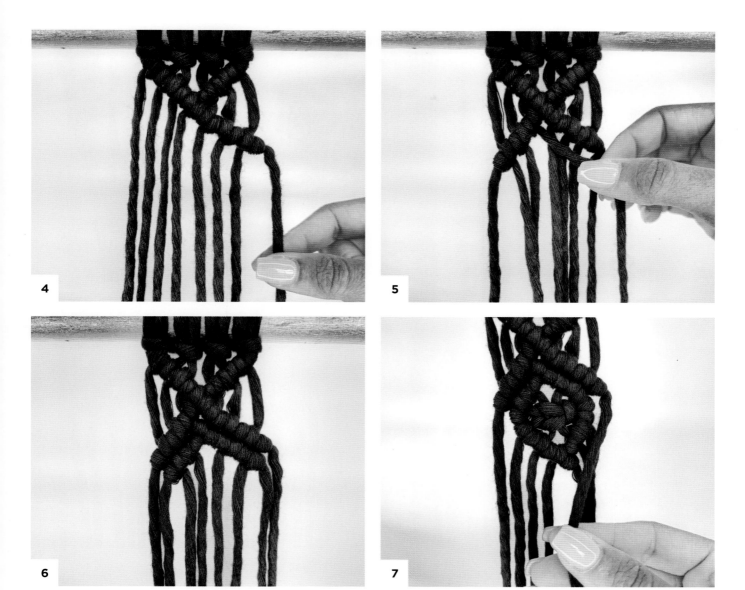

Four

As you continue to the right, have your working cord create a slight angle upward. This will make your diamond pattern slightly crooked and will help when attaching later.

Five

Continue your knots to the left, creating a slight angle downward. Then find the inner top left cord.

Six

With the inner top left cord, continue making double half hitch knots to the right. Repeat this on the left.

Seven

You should have two rows of double half hitch knots. Add a square knot in the middle and close your diamond. Next you'll continue your knots starting on the right.

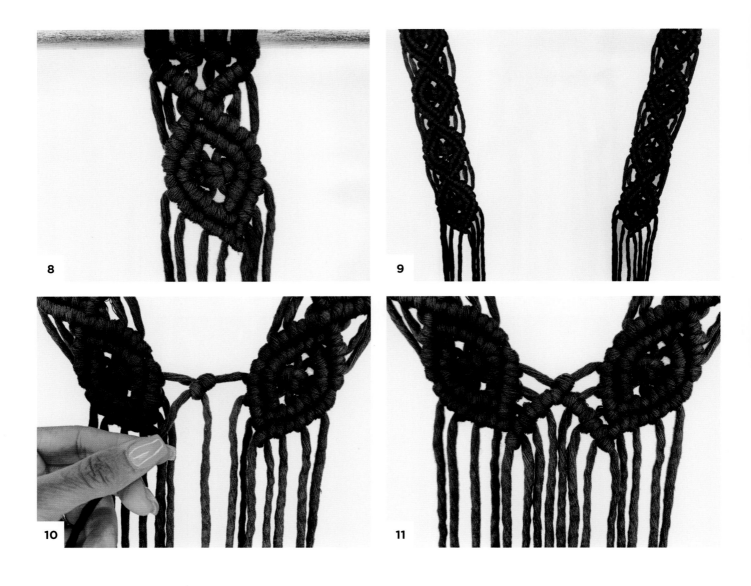

Eight

Continue your knots on the left. Close your outer diamond by attaching the working cords.

Nine

Continue creating your diamonds until you have four on each section.

Ten

Bring your sections together. Attach the sections with the inner top cords with a double half hitch knot, leaving about ½″ (1.3 cm) on each side of the knot.

Eleven

Continue your knots to the left to the bottom of your final diamond. Repeat this on the right side.

Twelve

Finish the diamond as you did in steps six and seven.

12

Thirteen

Repeat steps two through twelve to add the pattern on the right, leaving about 1″ (2.5 cm) between the two inner groups of cords at the top of the dowel.

Add two more sections of four with your remaining 15′ (4.6 m) cords. Make sure each section is centered over your attached sections.

Fourteen

Add a traditional diamond pattern, adding a bead to the center, and closing the diamond around the bead.

Fifteen

Continue this until you have six diamonds in each section.

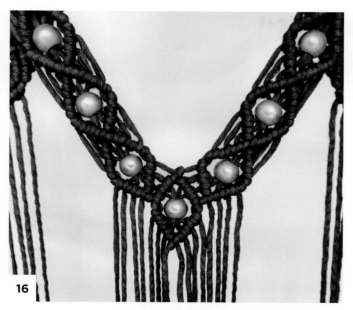

Sixteen

Bring the two beaded sections together and add a diamond pattern as you did with your other sections, adding the bead to the center.

Seventeen

Fold one of your 41″ (104 cm) cords in half. Put the loop through the back of the outer right section.

Eighteen

Attach the cord with a lark's head knot.

Nineteen

Repeat to add two more cords.

20

21

22

Twenty

Repeat these steps to add three cords to each outer section on both sides of the wall hanging.

Twenty-One

Add two of your 12½′ (3.8 m) cords to the right of your work. Add half square knots until the section is about 17″ (43.2 cm) long.

Twenty-Two

Add a bead to the bottom. Brush out the fringe and trim the ends again where you'd like. Then trim the ends of your piece and shape how desired.

Twenty-Three

Repeat steps twenty-one and twenty-two on the other side to complete your wall hanging.

23

Ombre Fruit Basket

Once finished, this fruit basket will measure about 36″ (91.4 cm) in length. I created an ombre effect with my colors and chose some neutrals that would look great in most kitchens.

Tools, Materials & Knots Needed

We'll be using 4mm zero-waste single strand cotton cord in this project. I've used the following:

Ivory

Natural

Moon

Taupe

SUPPLIES:

Four 17½′ (5.3 m) cords, ivory

Four 17½′ (5.3 m) cords, moon

Forty-eight 36″ (91.4 cm) cords, natural

Sixty-four 36″ (91.4 cm) cords, taupe

One 12″ (30.5 cm) cord, ivory

One 12″ (30.5 cm) cord, natural

One 12″ (30.5 cm) cord, taupe

Metal ring

Two metal circle frames, 8″ (20.3 cm) and 10″ (25.4 cm) diameter

Scissors

Tape measure

OPTIONAL:

Garment rack

S hook

KNOTS:

Lark's head knot

Half square knot

Alternating square knot

Gathering knot

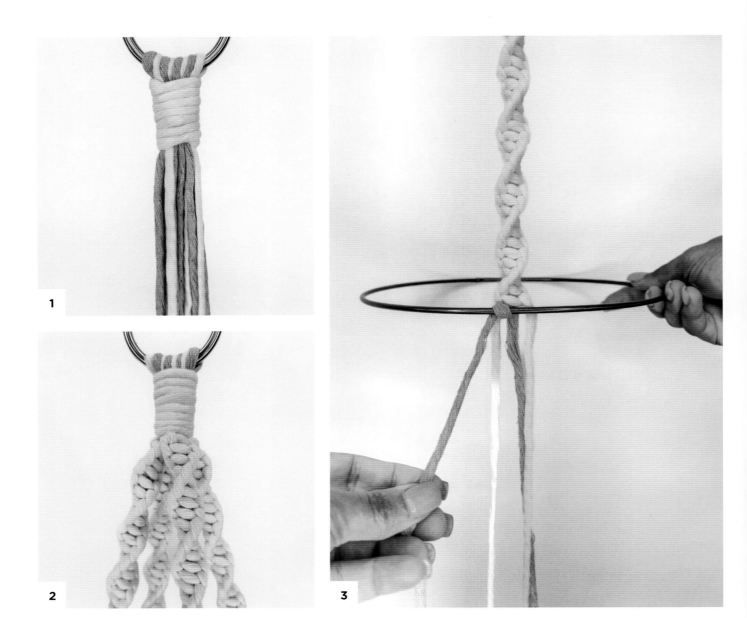

One

Thread your 17½′ (5.3 m) ivory and moon cords through your metal ring, alternating each color. Use your 12″ (30.5 cm) ivory cord to add a gathering knot below your ring.

Two

Add half square knots with your ivory cords over your moon cords, until each section is 14½″ (36.8 cm) long.

Three

Next you'll attach your 8″ (20.3 cm) metal circle using the moon cords. All of your cords should be inside the circle. Find the left moon cord and pull the cord around and up, wrapping around the circle to the left.

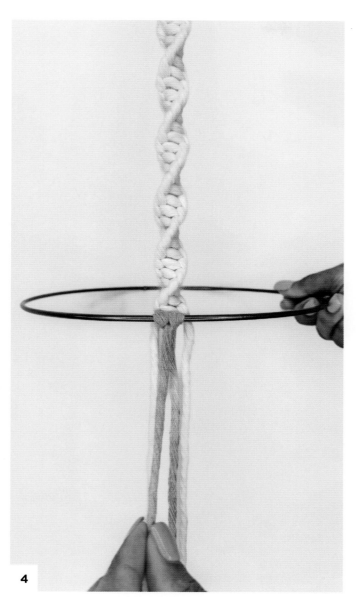

Four

Wrap around again and pull the end of the cord through the loop and pull tight. Repeat this with the right moon cord.

Five

Repeat steps three and four with each moon cord, making sure each section is evenly spaced around the metal ring.

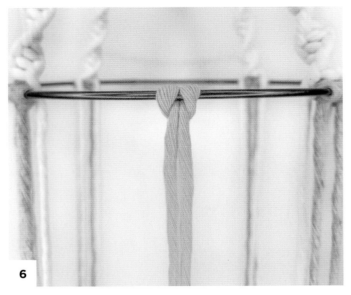

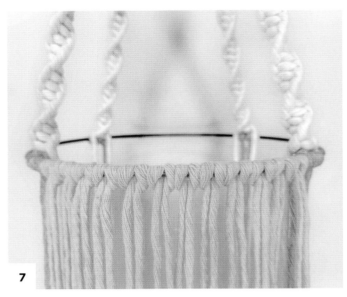

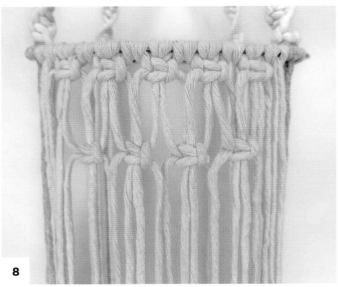

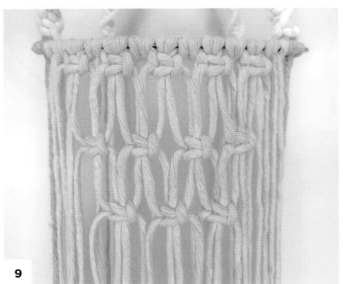

Six

Fold your 36″ (91.4 cm) natural cord in half and place the loop behind your circle. Attach using a lark's head knot.

Seven

Continue adding your cords. You should have twelve in each section.

Eight

Skipping your outer lark's head knots, add a row of square knots. Add a row of alternating square knots 1½″ (3.8 cm) below.

Nine

Add a third row of alternating square knots 1″ (2.5 cm) below.

10

11

Ten

Returning to the outer lark's head knots you skipped in step eight, add a square knot with your skipped cords. Make sure your ivory and moon cords are left out—you'll need them later.

Continue your rows of alternating square knots all the way around your work.

Eleven

Add a fourth row of knots 1″ (2.5 cm) below, using three of your upper knots. These knots should have six cords inside.

Twelve

Gather all your cords and add a gathering knot directly below your fourth row of square knots, using your 12″ (30.5 cm) natural cord. Trim the ends where desired.

Thirteen

Next you'll continue your spiral pattern with the moon cords. Add half square knots with your moon cords over your ivory cords until each section is 11″ (27.9 cm) long.

Fourteen

Add your 10″ (25.4 cm) circle using the moon cords.

Fifteen

Add the taupe cords to the circle using lark's head knots. There should be sixteen cords in each section.

Add a square knot with your skipped cords on top of the ivory and moon cords this time.

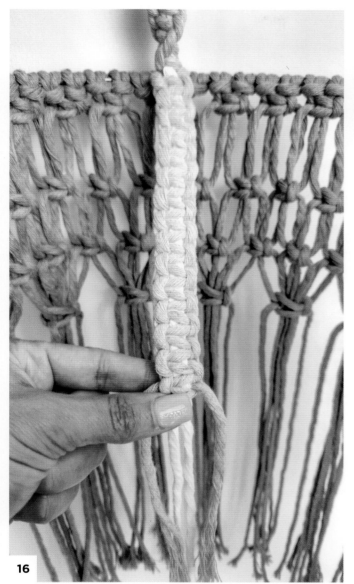

Sixteen

Add rows of alternating square knots as you did in the upper section. On the inside of the circle, using the moon cords, add square knots over the ivory cords. This should be 6″ (15.2 cm) long.

Repeat this on each section.

Seventeen

Add a gathering knot with your 12″ (30.5 cm) taupe cord and trim where desired.

Disco Ball Hanger

Let's learn how to create a hanging without the tail! The best part about this style is not only is it super easy and quick, it also can be used as a plant hanger. When finished, your hanger will measure about 36″ (91.4 cm) long and hold a medium-sized disco ball.

Tools, Materials & Knots Needed

We'll be using 3mm metallic twist cord in this project. I've used the following:

Rainbow

SUPPLIES:

Five 7′ (2.1 m) cords

One 2′ (0.6 m) cord

Two 2″ (5 cm) metal rings

Scissors

Tape measure

OPTIONAL:

Hot glue gun

Garment rack

Two S hooks

KNOTS:

Lark's head knot

Gathering knot

Overhand knot

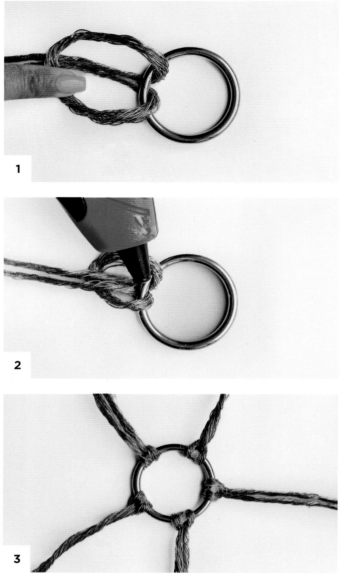

One

Working on a flat surface, fold one of your 7′ (2.1 m) cords in half and place under one of your metal rings. Fold over the loop and add a lark's head knot, but don't pull it tight.

Two

This part is optional but recommended. Add a bead of hot glue on your ring in the middle of your knot before closing the knot.

Three

Repeat with your remaining cords, spacing them evenly around the ring. Let dry.

Four

Add the ring to your S hooks, ensuring the ring is parallel with the floor. Find the right cord from one section and the left cord from the next. Attach them with a traditional overhand knot about 6″ (15.2 cm) from your ring.

5

6

Five

Repeat this in each section, ensuring the knots are even with each other. You should have five knots.

Six

Repeat steps four and five about 4″ (10.2 cm) down from your knots. You should have five more knots.

7

8a

Seven

Remove from your S hooks and flip over. Your metal ring should now be at the bottom, parallel to the floor. Add your second metal ring to the S hook. Thread four of your cord ends through the front of the metal ring, and the other four through the back. Adjust them as needed to ensure your bottom ring is still parallel to the floor and the length of the hanger is where you want it.

Eight

Gather the cords below the top metal ring. Add a gathering knot with your 2′ (.61 m) cord. Trim the ends, leaving about 3″ (7.6 cm) exposed, being extra careful not to cut your main cords.

Ensuring the Proper Fit

The length between your knots determines what size disco ball or plant your hanger it can hold. The smaller the item, the closer you'll want to put your knots. Before adding your gathering knot, and while holding your cords tightly, add your item to make sure it will fit properly. Redo the knots as needed to make sure it's a perfect match!

8b

Maroon Earrings

These earrings will measure about 6″ (15.2 cm) in length.
Feel free to substitute cord color(s) and beading.

Tools, Materials & Knots Needed

I've used maroon 2mm bamboo yarn in this project. I chose to use the bamboo yarn to add shine. You can use 2mm single strand macramé cord for these earrings.

SUPPLIES:

Six 12″ (30.5 cm) cords

One 6″ (15.2 cm) cord

Two gold beads

Two teardrop-shaped metal earring findings, or the shape of your choosing

Gold jump rings & earring hooks

Scissors

RECOMMENDED:

Cork trivet & pins

Knitting needle

KNOTS:

Lark's head knot

Double half hitch knot

Gathering knot

One

Fold a 12″ (30.5 cm) cord in half and place the loop behind your earring. Attach the cord with a lark's head knot.

Two

Add the remaining 12″ (30.5 cm) cords.

Three

Add half hitch knots to the right.

Four

Add half hitch knots to the left and attach your working cords.

Five

Add only one half hitch knot going to the right. (You can pin the earring down to a cork trivet at this point to help keep everything steady.)

Using both that cord and your working cord, continue adding half hitch knots over both cords. The two cords should be your working cords.

Six

Repeat this on the other side, and attach your working cords with one cord.

7

8

Seven

Continue this process until you have four rows.

Eight

Turn the earring over and add a gathering knot with your 6″ (15.2 cm) cord. Trim and hide the ends of the gathering knot.

9

10

Nine

Trim the ends where desired. Then prepare to add a bead. I separated a string from the yarn and threaded it through the bead. You can do this with macramé cord as well. You're going to add the bead to the center of your first row of knots.

Ten

Thread your string through, using the recommended knitting needle if necessary. Secure with a double or triple knot on the back side of the earring. Add your jump rings and earring hooks. You can also brush out the fringe if you like a tasseled look.

Repeat steps one through ten to create the second earring.

Rainbow Wall Plant Hanger

This plant hanger will hold a small- to medium-sized pot. The pot photographed is 5″ (12.7 cm) tall and 5″ (12.7 cm) in circumference.

Tools, Materials & Knots Needed

We'll be using 4mm zero-waste single strand cotton cord in this project. I've used the following:

Red amber

Copper

Ocher

Heather sage

Navy

Maroon

Ivory

SUPPLIES:

Twelve 12½′ (3.8 m) cords, two of each rainbow color

Twelve 12½′ (3.8 m) cords, ivory

One 12″ (30.5 cm) cord, ivory

Wood dowel, 5/8″ x 12″ (1.6 x 30.5 cm)

Scissors

Tape measure

Pet brush or fine-tooth comb

OPTIONAL:

Garment rack

S hooks

KNOTS:

Lark's head knot

Alternating square knot

Double half hitch knot

Gathering knot

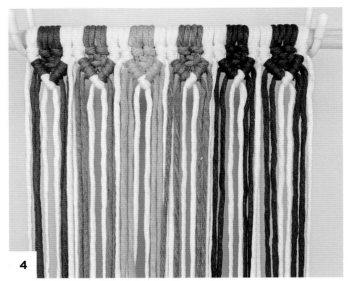

One

Add your cords to the dowel in rainbow order, using lark's head knots, with one ivory cord on the outside ends and two ivory cords between each color. Make sure your center ivory cords are centered on your dowel.

Two

Add a row of square knots with your colored cords only.

Three

Starting with the far left ivory cord as your working cord, add a line of double half hitch knots going to the right to the bottom of your square knot.

Four

Repeat this on the right side of your square knot and attach the working cords. You should have a "V" shape around your square knot. Repeat this with each color.

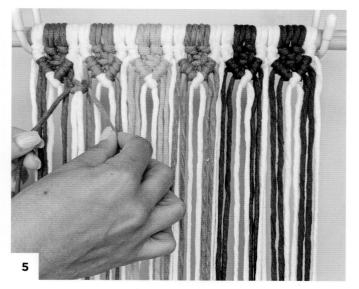

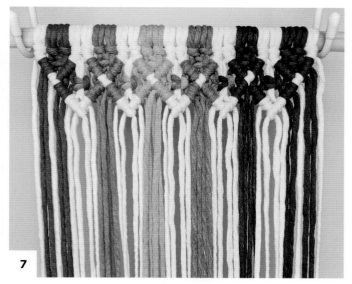

Five

Add a square knot using your innermost red amber and copper cords.

Six

Repeat this with each color. Using the far left ivory cord as your working cord, add a line of double half hitch knots going to the right to the bottom on your square knot.

Seven

Repeat on the right side of your square knot and attach the working cords. You should have a diamond shape around your square knot. Repeat this with each color.

Eight

Continue this process until all the alternating square knots have diamond shapes around them.

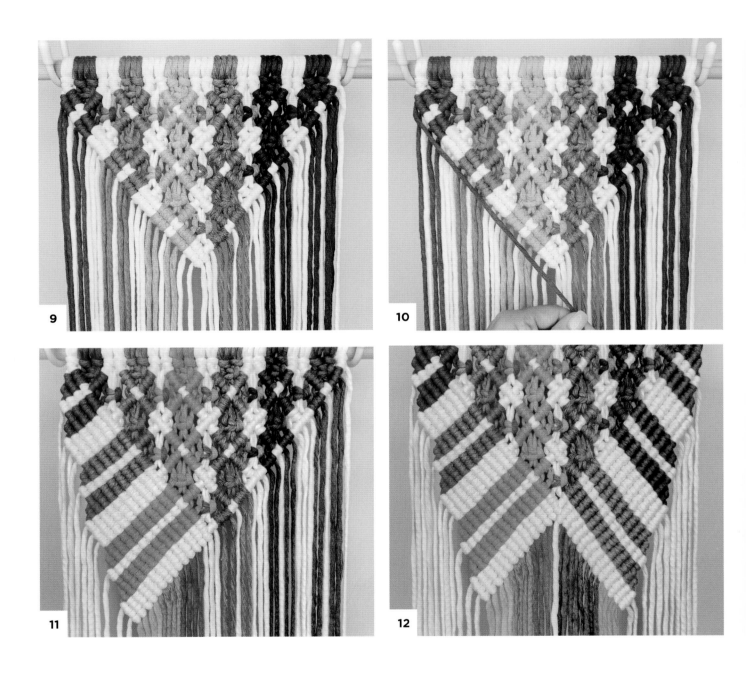

Nine

Using your far left ivory cord as your working cord, add a line of double half hitch knots all the way down to the center of your piece.

Ten

Repeat with the far left red amber cord.

Eleven

Continue with only the colored cords, skipping each ivory cord. The ivory cords should hang to the outside, with the colored cords on the inside.

Twelve

Repeat this on the other side

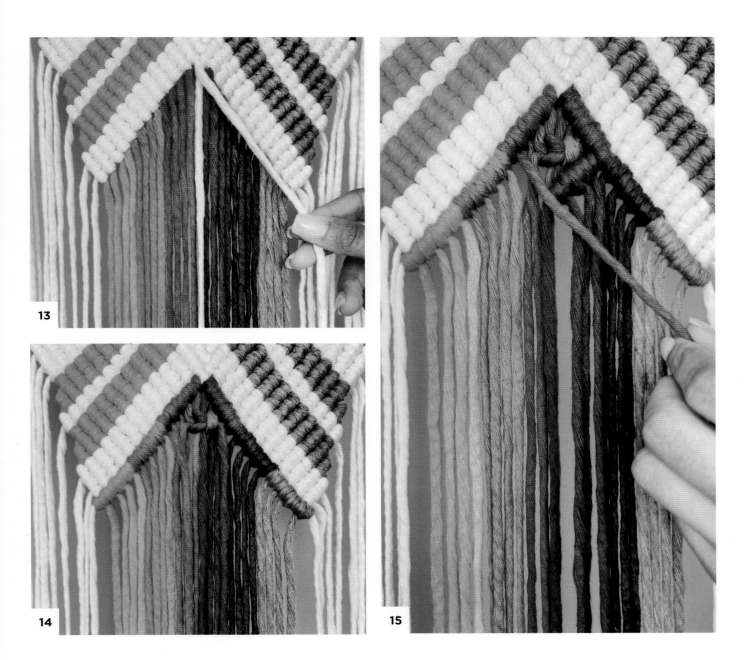

Thirteen

Find your inner left ivory cord. This will be your working cord. Add a line going to the right of double half hitch knots with the colored cords.

Fourteen

Repeat this on the other side. Then add a square knot with your inner red amber and maroon cords.

Fifteen

Add a line of double half hitch knots going to the left with your bottom maroon cord.

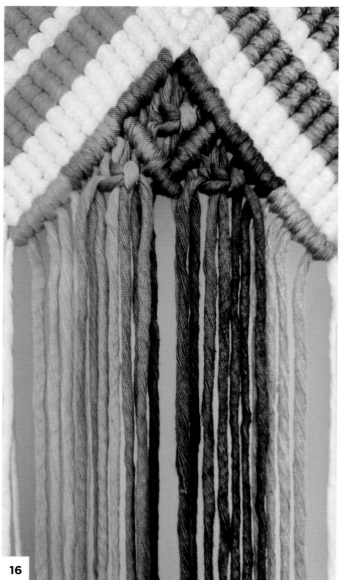

Sixteen

Repeat this going to the right with your bottom red amber cord. Attach your working cords to finish the diamond around your square knot.

Add a row of square knots with your copper-and-red amber and maroon-and-navy sections.

Seventeen

Add double half hitch knots, creating diamonds around your square knots. Continue this process with each set of colors, adding diamonds around your square knots. Close the bottom of your large diamond with the ivory cords.

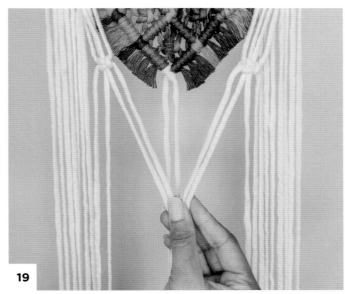

Eighteen

Trim your colored cords, leaving about 1″ (2.5 cm) length. Brush the fringe out and trim again as desired.

Nineteen

Using your far left cords, add a square knot 13″ (33 cm) down from your dowel. Repeat this on the other side.

Pull the outer two cords of each square knot around and toward each other.

Twenty

Add a square knot 2″ (5 cm) down from your top row.

Twenty-One

Find the outer two hanging ivory cords. Attach with a square knot to your top row of knots 2″ (5 cm) down. Repeat this on the other side.

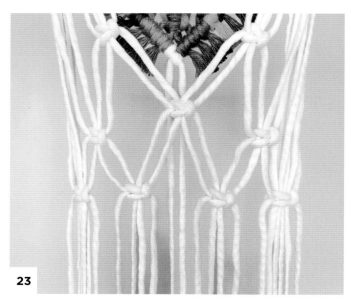

Twenty-Two

Find your four left hanging ivory cords and pull around toward the front of your work. Add a square knot about 1½″ (3.8 cm) down. This knot should have three cords on the inside.

Twenty-Three

Add a square knot to its right, making sure it's level. Repeat on the other side.

Twenty-Four

Turn your work around. Add a square knot with your four hanging cords. This knot should be level with your front center knot.

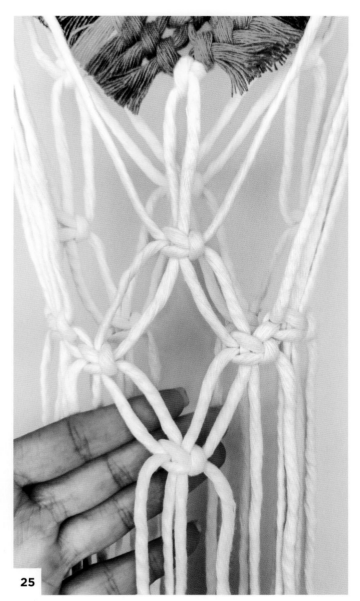

25

26

Twenty-Five

Add a row of square knots attaching the front and back directly below your front third row. Attach those knots with a square knot in the center about 1½″ (3.8 cm) down.

Twenty-Six

Gather your cords and add your pot, leveling where you'd like it to sit. Remove the pot without removing your hand. Add a gathering knot with your 12″ (30.5 cm) ivory cord. Trim where desired.

You can add a hanging cord by adding constrictor knots to the dowel. Or you can hang this using two cup hooks.

Suppliers

Yarn & Cord
2mm zero-waste 3 ply cotton rope, 2mm bamboo yarn, 4mm single strand macramé cord
Ganxxet
ganxxet.com/discount/caseyalberti

Scissors
LDH Scissors, Ldhscissors.com

Metal Circle Frames & Earring Findings
Unfettered Co
Etsy.com/shop/unfetteredco

Metallic Cord
3mm metallic cord
Lifetime Buttons LCA
Etsy.com/shop/lifetimebuttonslca

Clothes Rack & Cork Trivet
Ikea.us.com

Wood Dowels
Lowes.com

Additional Supplies
Lamp frame, crystals, gold leaf, wood rings, metal rings, S hooks, pet brush, fabric stiffener & beads
Amazon.com/shop/sweethomealberti

About the Artist

CASEY ALBERTI BEGAN HER MACRAMÉ JOURNEY in the fall of 2019 following a personal tragedy. She was looking for something creative that could keep her hands busy and her mind quiet. After making a few plant hangers, she was hooked! She started her business, Sweet Home Alberti, and has been blown away by the success. Casey loves to use color to turn something ordinary into something striking. Macramé has shown her that everyone has an artist in them. And that healing isn't linear, but for her, fiber art can provide structure in times of uncertainty. She's inspired by art deco, color, plants, and her supportive online community.

Casey has been featured in Etsy's blog, *Good Housekeeping*, eHow, and more.

She lives in the beautiful Pacific Northwest with her husband and four children. She enjoys journaling, travel, and exploring to ignite her creativity.

You can find more of Casey's work on Instagram, @sweethomealberti, or on her website, www.sweethomealberti.com

Acknowledgments

FIRSTLY, TO MY BEAUTIFUL HUSBAND ANTHONY, thank you. None of this would be possible without your unwavering support. Thank you for encouraging me, picking up the slack when needed, and reminding me that I'm capable of more than I know.

To my best friend, photographer, and stylist, Christine Shields—I couldn't live without you. Thank you for helping me turn this book into exactly what I had envisioned. Your talent inspires me and I'm so grateful I get the honor of calling you my oldest and dearest friend. Thank you for always showing up for me.

To my queens: Whitney, Lena, Aurora, and Nosse—you all are the only reason I kept going. Thank you for keeping a safe space and cheering me on.

Thank you to my sister Tiffany, friends, family, and kids. Your love and support always fills me up when the burnout is real. Thank you for being my strength.

And most importantly, thank you to YOU. I never believed that an artist lived within me. Without the support of my customers and followers, I wouldn't have found the courage to find the talents that have always lived within me.